Towards

Sandy Skinner

All correspondence to the author:

Email: towardslife01@gmail.com
Website: www.towards.life
Facebook: www.facebook.com/Towards-100284768329442

© Copyright Sandra Skinner

First Printed 2020

The right of Sandra Skinner to be identified as the author of this work
has been asserted by her in accordance with the Copyright, Designsand Patents act.

All rights reserved. No part of this publication may be reproduced, stored in or
introduced into a retrieval system, or transmitted, in any form, or by any means
(electronic, mechanical, photocopying, recording or otherwise) without the prior
written permission of the publisher. Any person who does any unauthorised act
in relation to this publication may be liable to criminal prosecution and
civil claims for damages.

This book is sold subject to the condition that it shall not, by way of trade
or otherwise, be lent, re-sold, hired out, or otherwise circulated without the
publisher's prior consent in any form of binding or cover other than that
in which it is published and without a similar condition including this condition
being imposed on the subsequent purchaser.

ISBN: 978-0-6485170-0-9

Proudly produced by

www.thebookstudio.com.au

~ About the Author ~

As a storyteller and an artist of words and image, Sandy has spent all of her life she can remember creating in some form or other. Creation and creative process flow easily from her, allowing challenging or simple conversation to emerge without a word spoken or thought. Big ideas can appear in lines, shapes and colours for her, as easily as a poetic line or pages of prose. Her creations allow her to listen to her voice and know deeply who she is and what she knows.

Sandy lives what she considers an ordinary life in Australia. She talks with people who do the same. For a long period of her life she tried to walk the road between being herself at work and understanding that she wasn't the one they wanted. Work required a certain mask that as time went on, the mask served less to protect her heart and more to complicate its need to be heard.

After more than 30 years teaching and living a full life, Sandy experienced post-traumatic stress as a result of work experiences and a life that had added its own versions of sadness. It was actually standing in her truth that 'life is a gift' that allowed her heart to welcome new understandings of old ideas and reshape the framework of her being to be, just be. That is what happens when it's time to leave something that has taken more time than family and other relationships in your life and you realise it isn't the relationship you want any more or can sustain.

So now is the time for **Towards**. The journal of how she kept going to work and bolstering resilience until it was time enough. Softened heart and kinder life are the pleasure of being a mother, a grandmother and a daughter; and very much young within her heart and life...funny how people over the age of 40 seem to need to add that 'young at heart' bit. Wisdom is the gift of life she has found and kindness to herself as love and choosing to matter.

Sandy now works as a life coach and speaker. If you would like to contact Sandy, please visit her website: **www.towards.life**

This is Sandy's second book. The first, ***Journey to Beautiful***, is a colouring book, but really a thesis of a journey from a small sense of self to knowing and accepting inner beauty and wholeness as it presents itself. The pages are her journal as the pages of this book are. With beauty came shifting and evolving as ideas mutated and new lines and images emerged.

'Within the lines of black and white is all potential. That is how I feel when I draw these pictures. Potential is seen and interpreted by the viewer, as much as it for me. Introducing colour brings interpretation and emotion for a particular moment in time. It finds the story and points the way to a feeling or an idea...Beauty is the wonderful gift of a happy and a peaceful heart.'

As an artist, this book was a wonderful way for Sandy to allow others to find peace and quiet to find their own stories. Sometimes they shared them. Everyone is living their own way to inner beauty and this is still a gift of time well spent with yourself.

If you would like to read some to the living to get to now, then 'My Sophist Garden' is her blog page: mysophistgarden.wordpress.com

Journey to Beautiful

Available through most online book suppliers,
or order direct from the publisher, Boolarong Press:
https://www.boolarongpress.com.au/product/journey-to-beautiful/

~ Foreword ~

Towards is compiled from parts of my journal.
My journal is my place to explore ideas and record moments
that touch me in words, in pictures and in open space.

Those open spaces, ideas and images are an invitation to you
to allow thoughts and feelings to arise within you
and join me in a journaling process that is leading you to
know what you know
and
believe what you believe.

If along the way something sparks a sharp feeling or a wound,
pause and see what it means for you.
Take the gift of time that you have given yourself
'being' in this book
and let it help you become the best version of you.

I don't mind what you think.
If you agree or disagree, I don't need to know.
That's not the point of being present with yourself.

It's all about you!!!

Action...write, record or draw your own story
into these pages with mine.
Breathe deeply and release a thought, hear your own voice.

To help you in this join-me-journal,
space has been intentionally left because I am giving you
explicit permission to make marks in the book.
Use it to serve you.
I would suggest enjoying a favourite place or drink as you do.
You are worth it!!

As the author I, Sandy Skinner, give you permission to:

Make notes on the pages any way that suits you.

Agree or disagree,
just know why.

Feel no guilt
over the time you take
to spend with this book.

Find the best parts of yourself
as you allow ideas to
play within you.

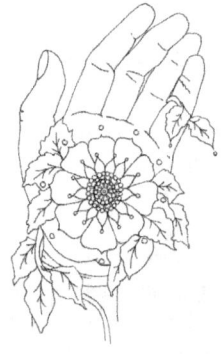

Please make your first mark here:

I agree to give myself permission
to do all of the aforementioned.

Signature:

and I get to live it.

Some say it is a set of lessons that we keep repeating until we find the right answer…but; what if there is no right answer only living. How do we know if we ever achieve them? Fear dictates looking for the right answer and looking for examples of what that might look like. It implies never right.

Some say it is a problem, or more pointedly 'I am a problem,' and 'I need to be solved' or 'understood'. The key to life is self-knowing.

Some talk of life as challenges sent to test us. Knowing of course we are never given more than we can handle so we will survive them all. Tests to prove what to whom?

Some talk about it like life is a sports match that we have to keep driving ourselves onward through. Greater achievement and maintaining our position in comparison to others seems to dictate the language that is used to talk about it. Words like expansion, growth, never good enough always more…

Some say other things…so many other things…
But what if, what if it is simply a gift. Every life is a gift. I am a gift. A gift to my own self and the people around me! Changing the words I use about my experience is the result of that notion. I am not a problem but a creative process that is responsive to the circumstances that present themselves. Like water flowing, changing its shape and force in relation to the landscape it flows over.

Life is a gift of wonder and tears and experience. Experiences that we all turn into some form of communication to remember, to share, to inform and to justify existence if justification is necessary. I think the fallacy that floats in the back of all minds is that somehow we are owed a gentle and privileged life full of everything we want and need with only positive feelings and knowing. There seems to be a growing trend to the idea that sadness and death should never touch anyone. Potential harm is on every corner and all potential fear should be planned for. For some people that is how life appears. Untrustworthy.

I have struggled at various time to find the light and joyful in amid the heavy experiences of life, just like everyone else. That is how I have encountered all these notions, paradigms of looking at life. There is now an industry out there built on moving ideas and schema around, I've looked too. Yet here is still what I know. This now is the gift of this now. There is no other now despite what we might think of it at any given moment. I think it all comes down to holding life in some sort of way so it doesn't seem to consume me but is lived with respect instead.

There have been times when it seemed like I needed more hands to hold what was happening but I only had my own. In those times I would look around me and open myself to another concept only to find it was really just what I had already encountered. In the beginning I thought that other 'spiritual' people might have something I didn't have. They spoke of experiences in a different way with other words. Over time I came to understand that I had known those same experiences just in different places and there was nothing new under heaven on this earth in the end. Some of the experiences they spoke of I had met decades before, the most confronting part of going venturing into other peoples ideals, they assume because my words are different or their words are like a special language to those that belong, that I know nothing and are somehow unevolved to their way and they seek to initiate me into their way by beginning with what is wrong with me.

Once I got past being 'put in my place' and negatively assessed by each group, I was privileged to look in and see how life was held in the stories individuals shared. I have always been the one other people told their stories too, big stories at bus stops or little ones throughout the day. All human 'hearts' it seems in my listening are trying to find their story of understanding of how it all works. What are they really looking for? Understanding enough so that life could be held and the painful moments held safely so they didn't consume everything else.

Life is a gift and I keep on saying it. Something gentle and kind has happened inside since the words started playing in my mind. Finally I don't need to contain my sense of being and simply get to explore life as my canvas and it will be as it is. I can't say I have ever been good at setting goals for myself. When situations arise I choose my way through it. Other people think it takes a long time and I must have spent many hours contemplating the course of my life but again that is not something I can say that is true for me.

Thought doesn't have to be a constant conversation to exist. I am not suggesting an autopilot type of existence, just one that I don't need to keep telling myself about. Some people need to hear their thinking and talk it through with others, maybe caused by the absence of others close by, but that has not been my need. I talk about things because people ask me. My self-reflection when it happens comes in moments of quiet when a big idea will appear, just appear in my head. Often I find I have drawn it already…not fully understanding the depth of the drawing or where my monologue is going, I just follow and one day I am there.

Perhaps this thing that happens, the exploring of creative process and touching of an idea has allowed me to trust my ability to manage most of the time. In my deepest, most quiet space I know I will be OK in the end. It is a sure knowledge that takes a lot of pressure off getting every stroke and line perfectly in place. I have painted pictures in many layers without any idea of what I was painting until I drew circles on the top to find dragonflies on bubbling water, and smiled.

> **I love that writing an essay like this, it is the ultimate moment of self-indulgence. I don't care if others agree with my words or ideas. I don't write to persuade.**

I love that I get to trust that my life will be what it is meant to be.

My life, this gift of being is a huge thing to hold; and quietly and loudly at times over all of the moments of living I think there is the image appearing of what it is that matters to me and what it is I hold and don't hold. This understanding is more than knowing who I am. Knowing 'who I am' is an easy part to achieve. Counsellors and all kinds of 'experts' will help you take a personality test to outline who you might be or you can listen quietly to the stories of your life and see your values unfold…

Peace is where I am. No need to apologise for my existence or prove I am worth the air I breathe. No need to be a great leader or better than others exists more than it does for any human. I kind of like that my life is quite ordinary. I love that I get to trust that my life will be what it is meant to be. I have the freedom of time to live until it is. There is no need to find the end of my life and live it now. That will come when I get there in time.

My language for now is what helps me understand or not understand (understanding is sometimes over rated) where I am on the map of day to day existence. I always know where I am. Sometimes I simply don't understand where that is in the context of the big picture because the map I am using lacks landmarks.

I followed a map like that once. The shape of the path was described but nothing much else was on the page like the farm I had to walk through or the stands of trees; let alone the peat bog with the one lone mountain goat that inspired a Sound of Music moment in my head. It was when I understood this concept. Oddly I found that I knew where I was on the geometric shape on the paper as I walked. Somehow that day it didn't matter. I figured if I kept walking and finding markers along the edge of the path I would find my way back to lunch.

I know where I am
I just don't understand
where that is.

Being Okay

Ordinary is almost a dirty word among so many people I know now. A quite extraordinary (sorry I couldn't resist) phenomena given this is Australia the land of my birth where ordinary was the goal and anyone else who might not fit ordinary needed to be torn down to conform to the ideal. Ordinary that I live in a simple house and go to work to put food on my table and petrol in my car. Ordinary in that I get to know the love of my children and parents and friends. Ordinary in that I get to love and create and breathe. It is wonderful to have nothing to prove. Yet there are times it still feels like it and I have to remind myself to breathe.

Born with different appearances and abilities, needs and wants what is ordinary as a base line anyway? Perhaps it is simply an agreed upon set of stands that allows the group to decide who belongs and who does not.

> My sense of ordinary is not the same as anyone else.

Today I look in the mirror and say
'I AM OKAY'.

When I said it, I know I meant...

On November 23, 2011 I wrote this statement on Facebook:

It is 4 months today that I have been here *(in the UK just travelling)*, away from my reality. I usually just make a general comment but today I need to say something more. It is by the kindness of strangers that I have begun to feel worthwhile and visible again. In the past week I have been engaged in conversations in which the other party seemed to want to know who I was, sort of like they were looking to find me, not just assume they knew me. It has taken me a while to feel like I am whole and worthwhile, knowing what I want and what I need to feel. This journey has so been worthwhile even though it hasn't always been easy to deal with always being alone. But the kindness of strangers and the generous way people have shared parts of their stories with me has enriched my life in ways they would have no idea of. So I am grateful and humbled by the life that has been and the future that is waiting for me to gasp at as I go round the corner (poetic and soppy I know). I am sure I am beautiful and strong and weak and wise and foolish enough to make life out of it...I so hope it is happy too. Blessings my friends from the fog and the cold.

Today as I write it is November 23, of now and I write in a document that another person may read one day:

It is still hard to live alone and mostly be on my own. It is still painful to walk openly and with lots of flaws. It is still the kindness of strangers that touches my soul and reminds me to be human. It is still the love of those that show their caring that make life more than it would be without them. People still gift me their story. Sometimes they ask me mine. I selfishly tell my story of me sometimes. I don't want to be lost or forgotten anymore, particularly by me. I am still sure I am beautiful and strong and weak and wise enough for everyday. I still hope that there is happy in this life for me. I still hope one day the ache of alone leaves but it is possible to carry. I still cry many days and laugh or smile more. I still am more than I was before and less than I will be. I am sure the future will be what it is and none of it really matters as today is as much as there is to be in. I write words like they can hold the meaning of my life and ideas and hope someone else will understand them. I think there are many words but really there are very few things worth saying in the end. Life is a gift and I get to live it and in living the gift is opened and the rest can begin...again and again and again.

Today I remember when I have received kindness.
I am grateful for...

Is knowing who 'God' is,
the purpose of life
or the beginning of it?

Does it matter?

Without context,
no elaboration,
just a pearl of wisdom
in an ocean of opinion.

Today I listened to find my wisdom.
I heard my...

There on the side of the mountain, standing tall in the rainforest - a tree of elegant proportion. Huge against the sky - rising among the giants.

She feels like a mother tree...in the centre of all the others, she stands... sanctuary, safety...solace... silence happens without request - response to a calm and peaceful heart.

I stood with her today and rested a while...

Shhh...

Something happens
when I am quiet.

Shhh.

I can trust myself to know...

In the morning over coffee
thoughts swell and whirl
like psychedelic
light dancers.

In the morning over coffee
I see how much
I could achieve...
how much potential
I have.

Today when I paused, I listened.
I realised I hold onto...

Knowledge

Can you benefit
from knowledge
if you haven't
first believed
that you have some?

Wisdom

Today I can believe I have knowledge I know...

Enough

More than enough
Not enough
Wanting more
Signs of fear
Holding on
Always wanting to be better
EQUALS
A need to love one's self.

Drawing in the breath of life
holding it hostage
not letting it out
all the goodness with in
stale air let out.
Holding it in
clutching it tight
stretching the balloon to
keep it from leaving
the feeling of all is well
the feeling of connection.

Afraid to be able to hold enough, not more
letting out might mean
being the same,
not more.
Fatter and fatter until
it all melds together and fights more and more
for the breath to get out.
It is not yours.
It is not mine.
Nothing can grow,
nothing can flow
among the engorged of the species
there is no power in holding onto
more.

Enough for the day
let go.
Know you have everything:
need does not exist.

Today I will edit the 'stuff'
I'm holding on to
that is too much to carry.

And now I can breathe
as the tether breaks
and I simply let it go.

Today I ask...

CAN I trust myself to be
<u>enough</u>
to live the life I am in?

DO I trust myself to be
<u>enough</u>
to live the life I am in?

WILL I trust myself to be
<u>enough</u>
to live the life I am in?

Well do I?

Change is a sign of life

Born to live and die we must be the one species
that doesn't get eternal is the collective drive
that happens with or without our permission.
Charles Darwin got it.
So did spritual teachers of all kinds.
As a species we just want to argue about how...

When is a butterfly most itself?
Born from the egg or fluttering?

Before death - it always was the same animal.

Our perception makes it different.

Heralding Change

Adapt or Die...

I choose...

Today I thank myself for living every day.
I am grateful that...

Over coffee one morning,
she was talking about her life...proudly!
In summary of her life statements:
Live without being an apology.
Be a positive statement of okay-ness.

Today I love myself.
Today I bless myself.
Today I show myself kindness by...

KINDNESS

is reason to be THANKFUL...

is reason to be KIND...

is reason for GRATITUDE...

is reason to LOVE...

is reason to be GRATEFUL...

is reason to know CONNECTEDNESS...

is reason to be GLAD...

is reason to be LOVING...

is reason to SPEAK GENTLY to another...

is reason to be GRATEFUL FOR ENOUGH HEART TO BE PEACEFUL...

is a FULL HEART.

I thought one day I would want to see what might be on the other side of nowhere and nothingness. I feel quite free now in the place of not knowing, nothing to know, nowhere to go. Just STILL.

Today I choose to
listen to the voice within
then listen more
when it stops talking.

Then I hear truth.

Who said life beyond this planet
has to follow the rules
that allow humanity to perceive it on this one?

Who said that is the truth we must find
in the quest for knowledge and peace of mind?

Who said you must force me to agree
with your point of view
for your thinking to be valid?

Who said life on this planet
must follow exact rules
and arise to a particular state of perfection
when perfection was never the intention
of this existence?

Who told you this is the thing to believe,
to trust?

Who said?

Did you?

Today I listen to
who the source of my beliefs is...

Judgement

The assumption
that what we read into
other's people lives
is true.

Assumptions
are generally based on
points of conflict
with our own
value bases.

Why do you give yourself
permission to think
the way you do?

About you?

About me?

Private lives in public places

As I sat beside another drinking coffee we muttered about life, trivialities and excesses; a family sits down at a table near by. All the rawness of their existence is exposed in that moment. The only boundary between us is a little space. Their private life in this very public space: sweet little boys, a mother, a father (A momentary smile for I have been one of them in another time and space).

Entirely lost in the their own world around the table, they engage in their part of the scene, oblivious to the eyes wandering in their direction. Unaware of the times past they have triggered memories of in the minds of we who sit muttering about life over coffee. My companion is touched by something deep in the pain of her knowing of a moment such as this.

She too has been one of them.

Words erupt from her mouth. Passionate pain in the deep knowing of a similar moment and words she had left over, unsaid. My companion wants me to agree with her but I can't, I don't see it as she sees it. Memories differ. She cannot perceive that I do not want to condemn the people before me. She sees wrong I don't see. Wants there to be a wrong that I cannot see there. Still she wants agreement from me that her judgement is right. That I should join in...but I can't. She feels right, righteous, absolute in her judgement; so full of emotion.

All I can say is I feel dirty.

I say I don't like to talk about other people's private lives in public places. I don't like to say things about them in front of them. (People have done that to me, and I know how it feels. I once lived my private life in a space others decided was public. When you live in that space the onlooker feels free to talk about you as if you can't hear them. They believe they have a right to interject into your life and speak words that may not be kind...it never feels right to me anymore.)

> But...

All I can say is that I feel dirty. Immensely uncomfortable, I don't like to talk about other people like this.

> She feels judged.
>
> Of course she does.
> (I am saddened about that).

Judgement begets judgement.

It was not my intention to judge her. I don't own her pain though I can feel it being thrust at me. I wanted simply for the barrage to stop and kindness to return. It was a human moment. An honest moment of privates lives pouring out in public places.

> She could be me on another day in another place.

Today I am sorry for the stories I have
told about others, instead of myself.
I forgive me. I forgive them...

Watching

Looking with intent.
Memory of details
from such looking,
put into words or image.
Requires non-attachment
to the scene,
non-engagement with
the living being observed.

Am I
brave enough
to look with love
into the
eyes of me?

And not look away?

> Go and find a mirror...

look into the eyes you see.

Mirror-dweller I see you
looking back at me.
Who can I see there
in the reflection?

Mirror-dweller there before me,
who do you see
looking back at you?

Stranger outside of myself,
so familiar, yet so strange.

Mirror, mirror, mirror
in front of me...
only in you
can I see some of me.

Through my eyes
looking out I see
only the edges
of the facade you see.

Today I can see me when...

Have you ever looked out
through your eyes
and understood that the physical being
that holds the space
for the looking to happen,
is like a mask?

The mask isn't for me
it is for you to see.
I can't see what you see.
I cannot perceive me,
I can only know me.

The me I know has no body,
just ideas, knowings from my
essential experience.
Those knowings are the most
concrete of all.
Abstraction occurs when you ask me
to manipulate them
so you can share them
from my perspective
within yours.

Difficult:

You want my explanation of me to match your perception.

(Don't do that to me!
Or do I do it to myself?...)

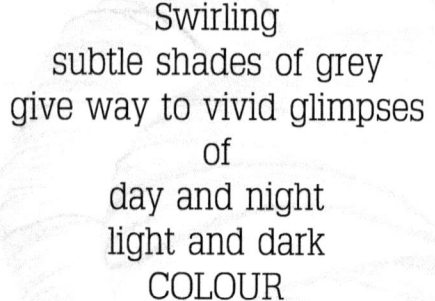

Swirling
subtle shades of grey
give way to vivid glimpses
of
day and night
light and dark
COLOUR

light
must
be bent...broken
to create hues...
the beauty we crave seeing
light from darkness
dawn

SIGHT

Partial truth
mixed with realities;
pieces of past
meet
fragments of future

Present erupts
from the living
of then
grown into
just NOW

...then...

A life and a dream,
an open welcome
to what becomes
vulnerable,
exposed,
fragile.

SOUL

Today some 'truths' stand out to me.
I allow space for them...

<u>Present</u> in this place,
regarding of light, colour, context
- present in this place, in time and space.

Hush.
Lost or found;
Present is the only way to know
where you are, how you are, why you are.

Hush.
Present to know that you 'be'.

Hush.
Present in this time and space,
hush lets you hear and see what is,
and what can be.

Hush.
Hushed and still
as the water puddles on the ground
and the rain drops dance more
to flood the edges.

Hush.
There is noise in the hush
when all there is just there,
and I pay attention.

Today when I breathed deeply
for just a moment, I closed my eyes,
felt my body then opened it to hear.
In the hush I heard...

Shhh...

Find the breath that leads to

HUSH

Shhh! ah, hush.

Moments of exquisite silence,
twitter of birdsong,
quiet clapping rhythm of the trees.

Echo...
Echoes...

Echoes in the landscape
now dotted with crow call,
dissonant rumble of modern life
drone to another timed song.

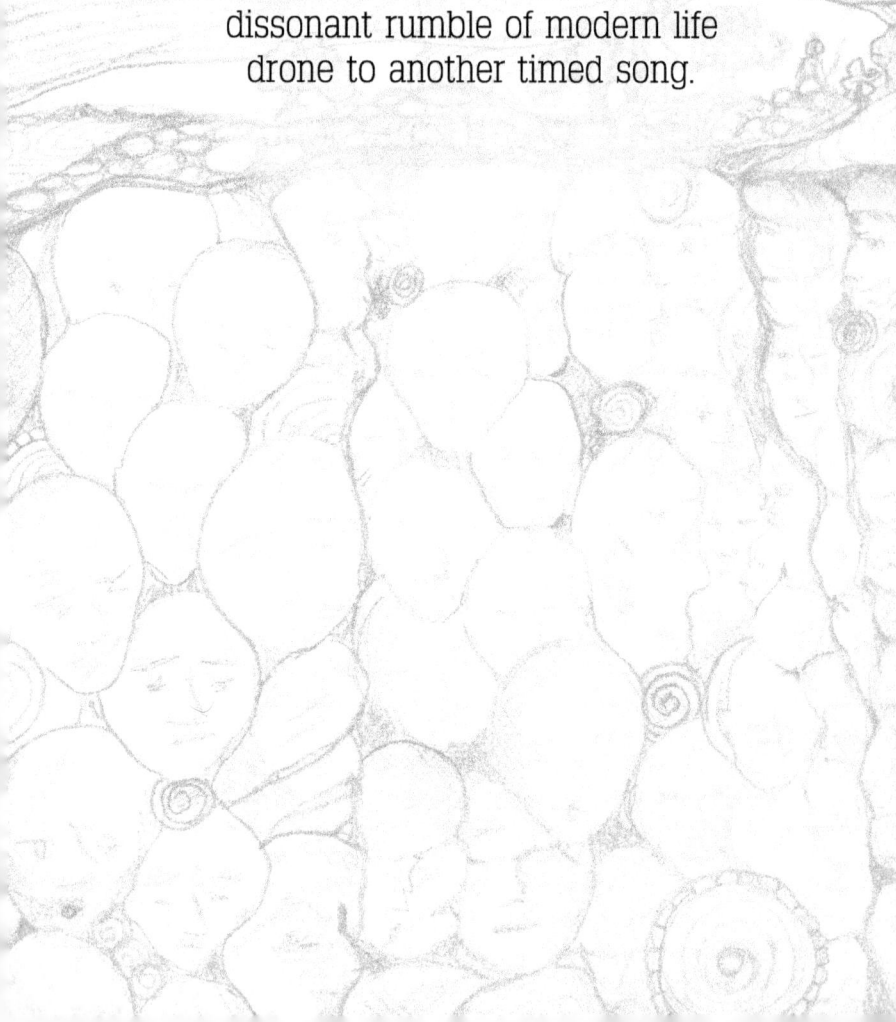

 Shhh...
Hear the echoes of life in the landscape.
No thing is without everything.
Listen to the fullness of the silence.
Be hushed.

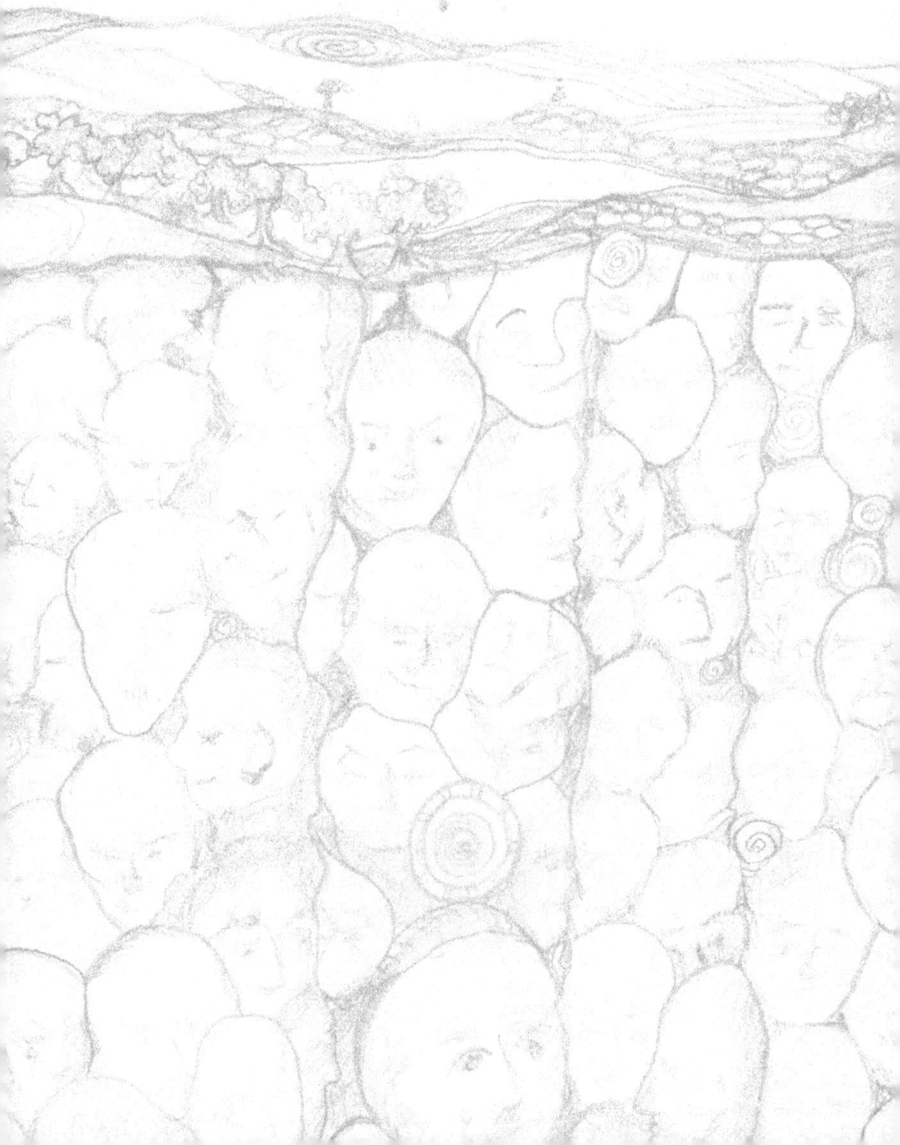

Consider:

In the beginning life began with a bang or a whimper or something in between but it began. When? How? Why? Scientists believe they can tell why and how and when now. The important part it is it began. Suspend judgement and observe the consequences.

It doesn't matter by what process we are here today though most beginning stories contain truth that science says happened. Science says it by endless hours of observing and questioning, testing and recording. Science began because humans wanted to understand how and why and when. So now we know.

Knowing doesn't seem to have helped humans to find contentment. Nor does it seem to have encouraged a greater sense of social consciousness. It seems there is a deep yearning for connectedness and validation that exists in all. Striving for evidence that would define human existence and explain why we are as we are still isn't satisfying.

I heard Jim Carrey speaking on one of those youtube snippets the other day. He was explaining his current place of peace and contentment with his life. I believe he was simply talking about being human. In the snippet he kept talking about how none of the stories he had told himself about himself really mattered in the end. They were just stories to hold his life in some kind of space in this existence.

Perhaps it is innately in all of us to look for why we exist. Science has helped with when we came to be as a species and how that happened. Why remains.

Does it matter?

Purpose. Purpose, the thing we are here for. So many words have been written on the topic. Religions have been born in the search for it. Arguments and wars fought over the *topic*. *Does it matter?* I don't know. Does it?

Most religions begin with why we exist and that is usually a brief statement that includes the idea that a power beyond our reality made it so. Most tell you there is an existence beyond this one that is better and should be sought...then they branch away to how we should live. The code that will let each one of us access that place without suffering, yet suffering is a part of living.

I personally like a relationship with a power beyond this one that I call God and how that God appears in my life. I like to read the wisdom and the not so wise-dom that has been written about God. As well as those who have tried to be absolutely sure they knew all there was and feel they are exactly right with God. I have also read those who have no assurance and no absolutes, mine is not a 'narrow-minded' perspective. In reading and experiencing I have a peace about where my life fits for me. *Can you say the same for you?*

Consider this then...

Do you have the right
to take away my peace
in your own right
to believe in your own?

Why does what I hold
my place in the world with
so challenge yours?
You want me to loose my place
and take up yours?

What gives you the right to think
you should do that to me
to make yourself feel better?

Today I let another stand in their truth,
while I stood in mine, when...

Because someone
who assumed authority
over my spirituality
told me a way to interpret
a set of words,
is no more valid than
the sceptic who perceived them
another way.
I have discovered that
the way I understand an idea
changes with life experience
and looking deeply
from other directions.

Perception

Those ancient stories
of beginning, exploring
and understanding
reference something
more than the tangible.
They explore the unknown
and unknowable,
yet there it exists.

The reason why living happened
the way it did;
seasons, weather, life and death...
data gathered by living,
used to try and predict or control:
to avoid danger and gain safety;
to avoid starvation and gain vitality.

Today I tell myself 'I am' because...

For the most part, 'how' we live
might actually matter the most.
I work in the field of special education.
A term I hate.
In the context of its pairing
with education, the word 'special'
takes on a meaning for segregation.

Among the people I encounter
when that fact comes to light,
the majority will ask...
Why are people born that way?
I respond in a manner to say:
Because they are.

Why is anyone born as they are?

Today I am grateful I was born as I am...

Knowledge and Wisdom

In the beginning
two trees in a garden,
two trees
not one,
two.

Consequences,
Possibilities
Enlightenment
Realisation
Angst
Loss
Living, finding, HOME.
Home to, not away from.
But...
to a tree in a garden
So very much home.

Today I visited a familiar text
and let go of what I thought it said.
It was then I heard it say...

In the earth I sit, of the earth I am.
Beauty and light radiate within and without
I have nothing to hide, no essence of shame.

Abundantly blessed
I have my heart to claim home.
I have my hands to build life and beauty.
I have my voice to chant my heart song...
I am as I am.

Little child you have seen many things, but have you seen a butterfly dancing in the breeze?

Have you heard a bird sing at the day's dawning?

Have you felt delight as raindrops fall to dance a moment on the earth?

Have you watched bubbles float, heard them as they popped?

Have you laughed at simple and magical little child?

Little child you have been touched by many things, but have you known the soft comfort of safe and loving arms?

Little child we love because we are loved.

In a world full of horrors that little child grows into adult to endure. Little child has the adult who is you still, remembered to smile today?

Do you remember if you listened to a voice outside of your own narrative?

Do you remember when joy at the ray of sunshine touched your heart?

Little child within your adult do you still feel and see and hear and know the wonder of being alive?

Little child with the adult who is you, do remember the voice of innocence that reminds you to love because you are loved?

Today I said to myself
'Little child of me'...

This morning
I wondered and smiled
as the bubble waited
and existed a while,
on a little leaf of May bush:
kaleidoscope of liquid colour
reflecting the entire world around it
in the singular form of the orb.

The fragility of the bubble
held the vibrancy of all
that was living within its
constantly flowing surface.
Within was without
and without was within
and within was without again
and again and again and again...
then not.

Blow a bubble at sunrise.

Today I blew bubbles and watched them float.
I saw, I felt, I understood...

Orb of dancing light
refracted into wonder.
She held it in her hands
and wandered to the place
of past, present and future -
In the palm of her hand
she held it.

It.

It,
The Secret
that only she in that moment knew.
Everything existed <u>not</u>.
Not even now existed,
only her.

There is a moment
when light dawns
on the horizon
and creation is caught
between inhale and exhale,
and time is paused in now...
when all there is to perceive
is everything
and beauty is.

Hope is expectant then.

Today I heard myself say 'I hope'...

Looking in,
looking out...

earth,
wind,
fire
and rain.
Time,
season.

See the world,
hear the wind.

shhh...

Just breathe now.

All the beauty
of everything that is
and could be
is on display
just for me
this day.

On a hillside above the town of Melrose on the Scottish borders I was bent on all fours trying to stand up. The path was a muddy mess as its name implied Quagmire Lane. It had rained on and off through the morning and I was determined to walk the long way round to ice cream.

However as life would have it the path narrowed from a lane to a line of mud snaking through thorn bushes. The bushes so close that a child could most likely have walked through unscratched, but me that was an entirely different experience. As I walked the clay built up in the tracks of my walking shoes turning them from all terrain tread into glassy slides. Slide I did...into the mud. So I was there on my hands and knees trying to stand up with nothing to grip my feet into and nothing to hold onto but thorns.

I did what I have been known to do. I cried. Then, I took a breath and sort of half crawled and stabbed myself with thorns to where the edge of the pathway was clearer. Still near the ground a glint from the sunshine caught the corner of my eye. A sparkle so tiny if I had been standing I would have missed it.

The smallest of purple thistle flowers that humans associate with Scotland was blooming beside my hands. Crusted in raindrops it was more like fluid crystal than plant. On top of the filaments of the purple flower was a butterfly, so small it was perfectly proportioned to the bloom. My breath caught; a soft stream of warm tears tracked down my face. Such beauty in that place in that moment of discomfort! Beauty, oblivious to this lumbering giant that was caught in her own distraction. Distraction stopped and present descended.

My heart was warmed as it realised that the beauty before me was there for me to see. It existed whether I saw it or not. It simply was. I was blessed because I could see it. It was for me and in that slowing action, I could take it all in. I understood that right then was just for me. I was under no obligation to share it or make it more than it was. Beauty healed a place in my soul that day that I could not have seen unless I was in the mud where it was.

As gentle as a whisper
day came, day went,
sun shone and life flourished:
seen and unseen.

Getting Wisdom

The dawning of realisation is a process within the gift of time. We can feel knowing comes in an instant but the dawning of understanding may simply be the result of getting there. Allowing pieces to come together and being open to the conclusion announcing itself when it does.

In a society that craves a way to instant wisdom, without suffering, respect for the getting there with time is often lost. It is frequently not trusted even in a culture that proclaims everyone is free to find their own truth… The rush to instant wisdom can have the effect of learning to spell a word without knowing its meaning or a reason to use it. One day it may, but if there has not been the living to understand the truth in the wisdom it will only serve 'getting there in the end.'

> The dawning of realistion is a process within the gift of time.

The gateway to wisdom is being sold in the market place. The shortcut to the Tree of Life and the effects of living each day as it appears. So much knowledge is accessible that it is overwhelming if all truth is real and needs somehow to fit together. Wisdom allows us to filter that knowledge and find the life that sustains and the ideas that hold it.

Time only matters
when we count it to give it
meaning. It exists whether we
notice or not. It exists as a
reflection of the natural order
of things. It exists because there
is finite reality that moves and
beats to sustain existence.
Without it, we do not walk
humanly on this earth.

Time is a gift.
The passing of time
is the opening of this gift...

Immortality:

Opposite
of mortality.

Striving for immortality:

A desire to avoid
the real process
of the human
existence.

Humans constantly seek to avoid
the implications of mortality
- not the living part,
but the dying part.
Though the quest to avoid dying
can lead to a greater point
of sadness.

To live to avoid, skews the focus
of perception to looking for threat
rather than the wonder of living.
A process that cheats the human heart
of the fullness of being:
ALIVE.

Making peace with mortality
allows...the opportunity
for something real to occur.
A change of focus can arrive
that ALLOWS a change of perception
to seeking living.

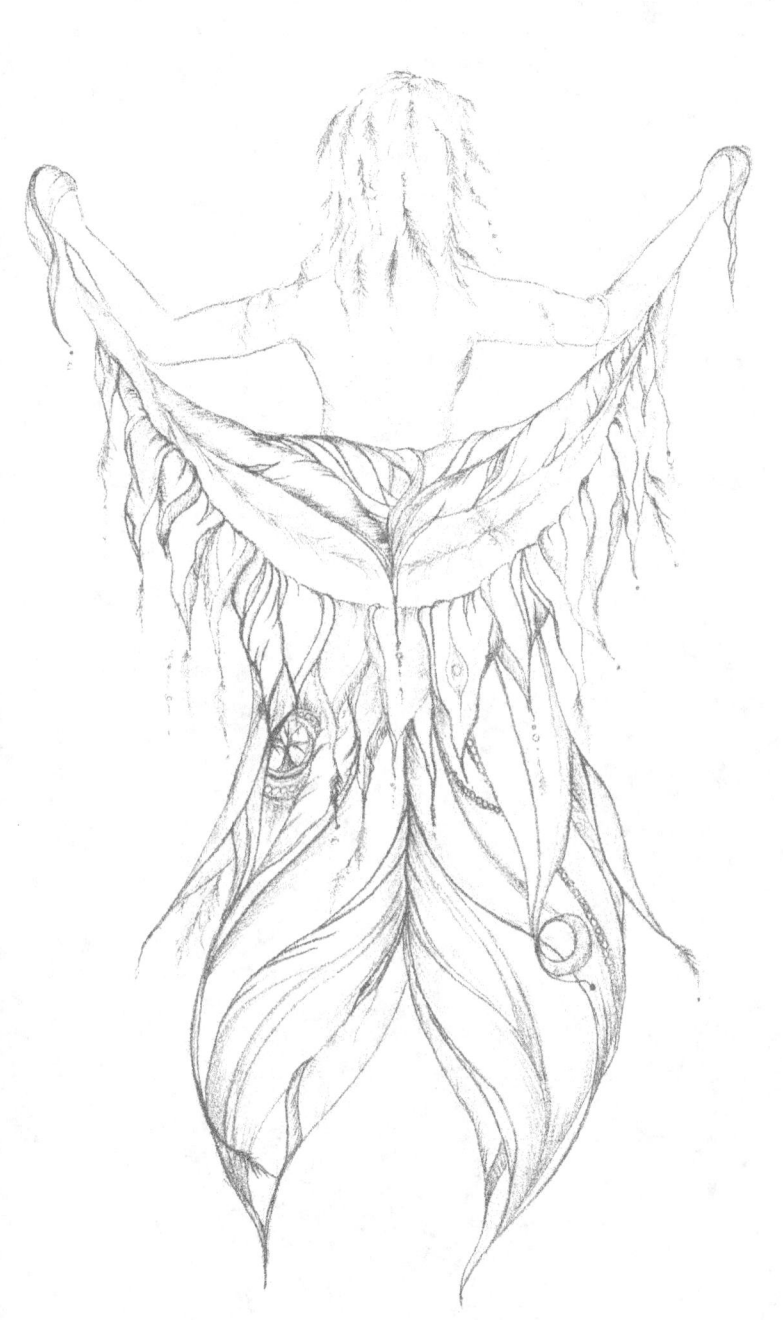

Despite all best efforts:

<u>Love</u> causes
grief,
which causes
inner richness,
which causes
<u>love</u>,
which causes
conflict,
which causes
negotiation and power play,
which causes
compromise,
which causes
peace,
which causes
<u>love</u>.

Not a hierarchy, but a swirling sea of reality
- all know it, but few understand it.

ALL of life, not just some of it.
All of life is the key to wisdom.

Tree of life...
That tree of life that
takes the soul back
to the beginning place,
that place of deep silence and knowing,
of self in the right way,
is still there.

Before surrendering to the temptation
to want to know more,
to want total control,
to want to be God
and ALL the resulting responsibility,
there was a place of knowing life
with ALL needs being met.
A quiet, still place:
The place with no words,
Only ALL.

Then NOW.

NOW is ALL there is.

I know where I am.
I know who I am.
I am...

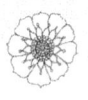

Validation

The sensation
of acceptable worth,
generally in the eyes
of another.

Okay-ness.

I am simply that I am.

Truth will appear.

Wholeness will take its form.

Humanness will be as it is.

I will be offended and I will offend
but I will love and be loved anyway.
Forgive and be forgiven.

I am and will be enough
for each moment of being.

Worth, respect and caring
will be as they are from me to others
and others to me.

Clarity will be when it is needed
and sometimes confusion
will lead to it.

I am simply that I am,
for I am a gift.

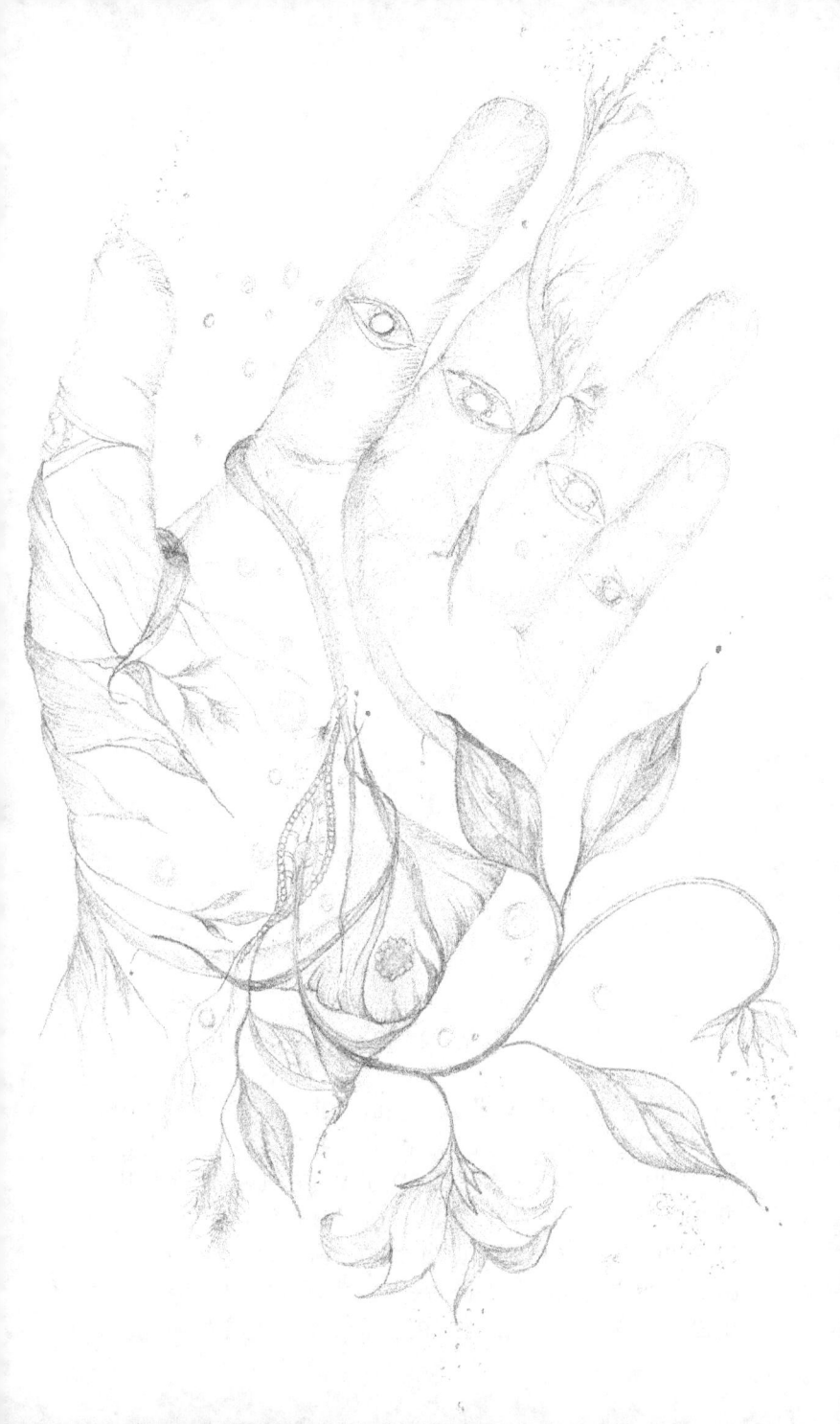

Impact

My words will have an impact and begin
a ripple like a single water drop in a still lake.
The energy of one drop of water becoming the
impetus for the movement of the ones around it, that
multiply the energy of impact and so it continues as
the drop becomes a wave, or at least a large ripple on
the shore. My hope is that ripple would be kindness.

Today I realised the impact of my words and actions are good and bad.

It feels...

Ownership of Reaction

The outcomes of my engagement in living
are not mine to own.
Like a painting that is becoming,
so the energetic, intellectual
and emotional flow from me
will become a part of something greater
than the beginning.

Your response to me is your response.
I have no ownership of that.
If you don't agree with my words
then you have many choices,
none of them have to do with me.

Right WORDS
Wrong WORDS
Left WORDS
Central WORDS
Popular WORDS
Disparaged WORDS.

Living among people
who always expect
the Right WORDS.
Want to hear their
Right WORDS,
Not mine.
So they do.
Out of my mouth.

Today I listened for familiar words,
seeking connection.

These are my words...

Reflection

What is perceived
in others as a
mirror image of self.

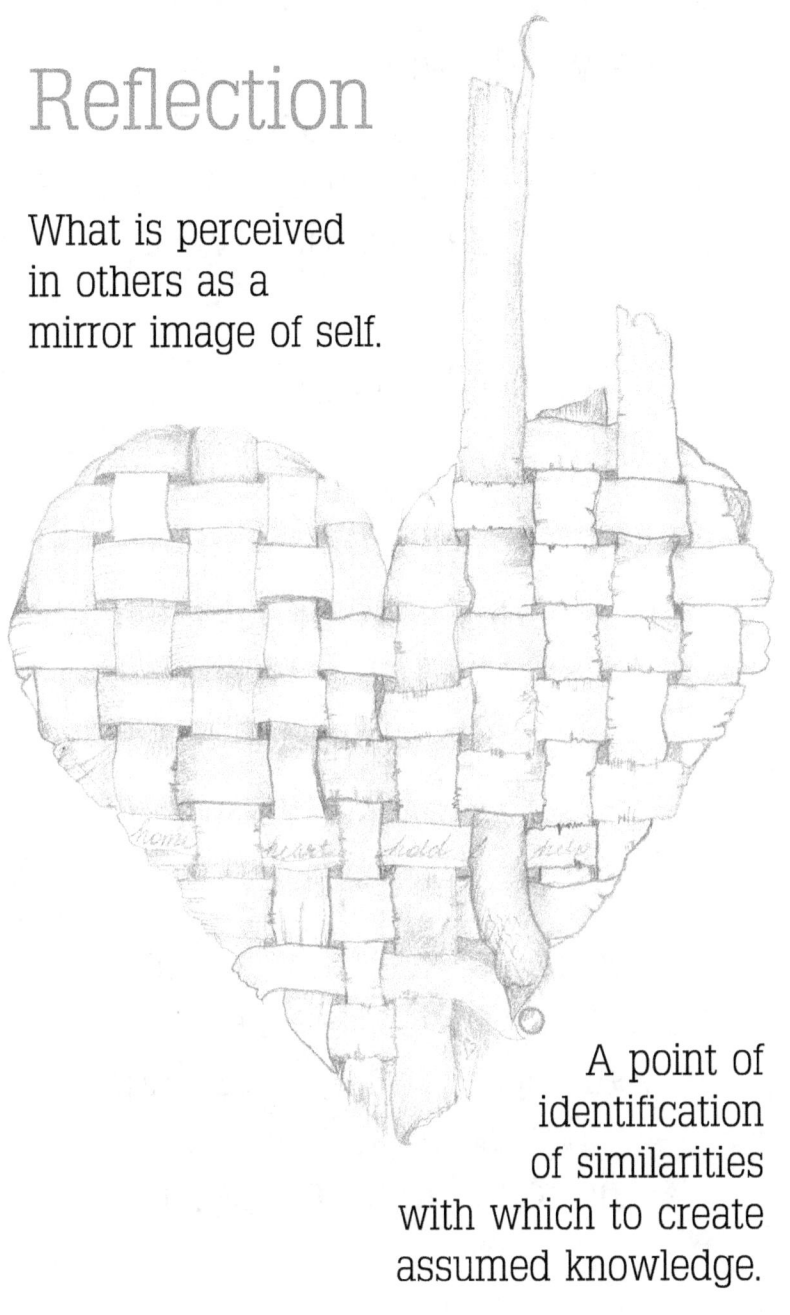

A point of
identification
of similarities
with which to create
assumed knowledge.

Little words with deep meaning
that are not respected
because they are simply little words
that seem ordinary.

Words

Little words...
little words of daily life
when eloquence and creativity
give way to efficiency of meaning
in hurried moments
without pause.

Listen to them
and the space in between.
See the face that spoke them.
Hear the sound of speaking,
the pace of breaths,
the tone, volume, speed.

Today I allow space for nice words
about myself.
So I say...

Do I have time for eloquence today?
If I take the time to listen to you,
will I have time to listen to me?

The questions we ask
shape the truth
we are looking
to find.

Why?

It seems to be the word that begins so many questions.
I am asked every day.
Everyone has a why question.
Children want to know how things work
or what reasoning was behind a decision or invention. Adults ask the
same questions but mostly they relate
to deficits and suffering (or the sense of it they feel).
Both want to understand the thing that is in front of them that they
can't put into the scheme of life they have
come to understand.

WHY?

Questions about the reasons why others are the way they are?

WHY?

Should understanding the actions of another
make me responsible for their choices?

WHY?

Should understanding the actions of another
excuse the consequences of their actions toward me?

WHY?

Does any of it matter?

WHY?

The question makes us human.

WHY?

Can you perceive truth
without asking a question
and looking for an answer?

You can't
hang a brick
in the air.

Meaning
has to do with
accepting
an assumption about
an abstract icon that
represents
a very concrete
thing.

At the table in the coffee shop she says,
"Ban the burka!"
She says this thing from behind her
wraparound sunglasses.
Wraparound sunglasses mask her eyes,
making them appear as blank pools of black
all over her face.
Blank pools of blackness
masking the windows to her soul
and obscuring her identity to me.
She is proclaiming that everyone should be seen.
"It hides her away from me looking in," she says.
"I hate what the burka stands for," she says.

?

The world isn't as it might be,
no matter which face covering you wear.

True colour
is obscured by
blank pools
of blackness.

Post-Truth

The notion of writing your own narrative
based on "facts"
that don't need a basis in "truth".

If everyone's truth is okay and right
then why do we need the term...
truth?

"People" gossip
and gossip becomes Chinese whispers
and whispers become truth.

What it becomes is the truth of the
people doing the speaking and listening,
but like all oral traditions,
it can change without effort
and the accuracy of the moment
compared to the source,
becomes irrelevant.

For truth to matter
it needs to matter
to you.

Narratives surround me
in every quadrant
with declarations
of what defines a perception
of what is concrete...real...
co-creation of an idea.

So here's the thing:
IS
The energy used on thinking
the <u>right</u> idea that important,
if every truth is true
and everything true to someone
is <u>the</u> truth?

Could Post-Truth be an era
of potential mis-truth
that becomes truth
as long as it is justified
by the agreement and analysis
of others?

Could it work like memories do?
I don't know if I have an answer.

Seeing in the Dark

The consequence of understanding is the dissolution of 'trust in' what was sure, because you question it. The desire for discovery leads to wanting more knowledge because trust isn't possible when responsibility for knowledge within self is the source. Dissolution of trust in familiar reality causes the departure of a known and safe existence regardless of the quality of that reality (Terrible has a routine of its own that allows existence and even when terrible is taken away there is a void). The leaving leads to awakening perhaps.

Awakening to?

That is what you choose to find. The choosing can be a repetition of patterns and finding the familiar with new names or it can be entirely other from what has been known.

Awakening is a loaded word as it has a perceived meaning among many that the individual will become more attuned to a particular view of the self and the world the self is in. Most often the assumption is that it will result in a kinder and better version of the individual as a response to the perceived understanding of a corrupt or harsh world. I have observed that people who call themselves awakened are harsh judges of who is of them and who remains outside the ideal.

Generally awakening is the thing that follows a sense of suffering or loss. It is the clarity of the after when the sufferer wants a new reality free of the things suffering brought. Suffering is like a grey cloud that seems to grow hard edges and become clearly defined. It casts a shadow* over a sense of the well-being in the sufferer's world and often feels overwhelming.

*SHADOW:

This absence of light is simply a void of perception.

Today I am awake within my inner being.
I am aware of new ideas...

Today I am looking at the odd shapes
of the shadows inside me.
I see an old story in a new way and I feel...

All attention is generally cast upon the shadow with little focussed on the source of light. And there is the ***subtlety of skewing***. If I am the vessel that carries the light then the shadow that is cast is caused by my light not a shape that is cast by me.

All Light is still Light.

Light enables the perceiver
to see in the dark.
Darkness is the absence of light,
which ceases to be
with the addition of it.
So everything that is present
is still there in either condition:
light or dark.

Perhaps awakening
is looking in the light
rather than squinting
in the dark spaces and shadows.

Everyone
wants to shine.

Everyone
already
does!

Like a star perhaps, or a candle in the night, or even a diamond ring, there is a desire in all the words expressed about life about being a shining example. Yet for most people there is a general sense of ordinary that is natural and normal. This world we live in adulates extreme achievement and great beauty; and elevates the downtrodden and impaired in their achievements. Being ordinary is not considered anything. There is no value judgment on this observation only that it is believed by some.

As humans we are a complex network of latent potential, life experience and processed information. 'Life' is after all experience which we turn into communication so we can share it with other people, and most often with ourselves. The experience of life doesn't happen in our heads that is simply where it is recorded as time past in the form of memories. Memories and self talk (communication) then frame life within so we can predict life outside ourselves and be ready for it.

Our desire for survival is so strong that we are always analysing and making judgements from the information our mind has in storage to increase our understanding of life and our ability to adapt to it. The desire for survival comes from the life force within. The desire for all things that we want in life comes from within. And yet we argue and angst with ourselves about judging what that should be.

STOP!

I stop.
I choose and allow myself to be loved by me.
I stop. It changes things within me...

I think it is from the inside out that shining happens. Like the circle with the centre from which lines can extend to radiate its shape, so we are. There are few that would find fault with that statement. There are many that would find fault with the experience of life that comes from that central being.

There is that question people often ask: Is the glass half full or is it half empty? Is there a deficit in the situation or is there a positive.

Most of the perceptions of life that I have listened to, work from the glass is half empty perspective. Many versions of psychological theory work off a deficit model, as do most religions and spiritually inclined belief structures. In fact it seems most of western society is obsessed with looking for how a situation, government or person is not as ideal as it could be.

An assumption exists that there is a perfect model that every person should be like. There are constant references to ideals about quality of people and life style based on arbitrary concepts of achievement and worth. It is perhaps one of the great sources of suffering that we accept in our lives. The belief that we are more broken than whole, sick rather than healthy, less than we can be for a reason we are not sure we even know anymore. You can hear it in the daily language of conversation.

We joke that we need therapy or speak seriously about needing healing if life isn't feeling right. We let practitioners of medicine and spirit tell us we are wrong without telling us how we are right. Words of imperative action are used frequently like 'I must visit...'; 'I should have known...'; 'I have to...'.

The words we use about ourselves **and our lives matter because they form respon**sibility and imply guilt where perhaps none needs to exist.

I stopped one day and pondered the idea:

I am
more whole than
I have ever been broken.

I am
more healthy than
I have ever needed healing...

I am...
I am as I should be.

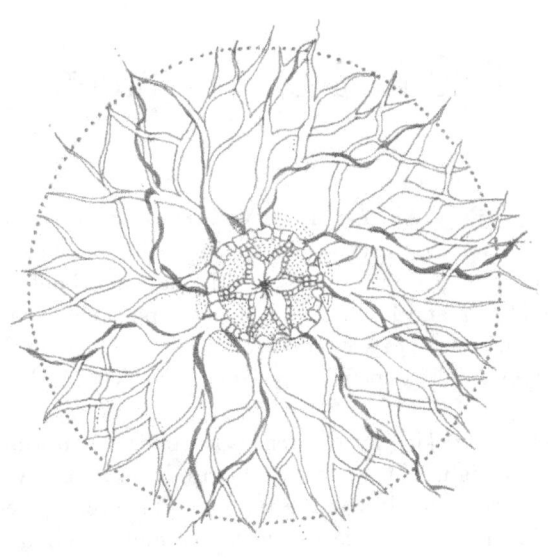

It is in being quiet within and touching my deep quiet place that has no words and is all gentle and strong, that this revolution of spirit erupted for me. Words matter from here on for me.

I do not desire 'medicine' for a broken life. My life is not broken it is simply life. Life is a process of experiences and I do not need to justify them only accept and journey through them. This is not easy. But then love is never easy, especially when I am loving myself.

However, change is something that happens in the now for the future not the past. Living in the past is something that is common among many people and all of us would be guilty of it at some point in our lives.

Being present in the here and now, by being attentive and focussed on the present is the simplest way to make different life choices. Know the past, understand what got you to here; but know that it does not have to determine your next thought.

Choose Non-judgement

If we are more whole than we have ever been broken and more healthy than we have ever been in need of healing for...what does that imply? It implies a resilience of soul that can be built on; positive attributes of self and life that can open up possibilities and lead to contentment. Instead of seeing ourselves as an enemy or ill to fix we have the opportunity to perceive our selves as able and 'ok'.

If you are only looking for the deficits in your life you will never see the wonderful light that is already there to shine. In a very real sense you cannot and do not love yourself. Love and Respect for self need to exist within for there to be peace and contentment in a human 'heart'.

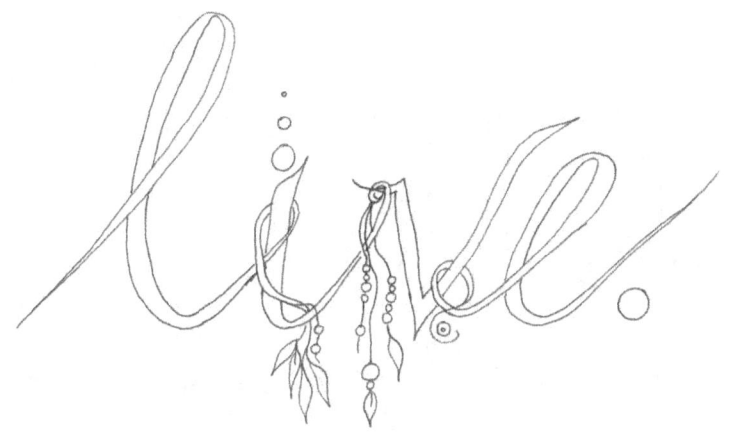

Allow
that life is a gift
then LIVE!

~ Postscript ~

In 2015 I concluded the foreword to my book, ***Journey to Beautiful*** with the words; *'Life is a gift, just colour.'* And in 2020 I began the opening pages here with the statement: *'Life is a gift and I get to live it.'* At the end of this book I repeat the heartfelt knowing, life is a gift, and encourage you to allow yourself to live it. Life is the only way we learn to love, to express ourselves as loving and loved.

Now at the end of this journey of words and images I am different, and you are different. I am open to allow another version of life and me in it because I have chosen it. I hope you are allowing the very best version of life for your loving heart to live too. Choosing to allow ourself to listen to what is our automatic ideas and patterns and pausing to offer our hearts and minds the opportunity to respond differently has required courage and commitment to write on the pages of ourselves, turn down corners and sometimes do some re-writing.

Now is when true brave and vulnerable hearts stand up and allowing the creating of the best version of lives for ourselves. It is a choice I have to make every day. It is held in the knowing I bring whatever my best version of me can be each time and sometimes that can be really messy. I am learning still to listen to myself, really listen. I am learning to love myself, really love myself.

It matters to find our loved being because without that being we cannot do as we are encouraged to love another as we love ourselves. We can only know a dim perceived notion of who we be, looking into a dimly lit mirror full of shadows. Light can show us who we are and cause the edges of our images to be defined and visible. Are we all brave enough to own our image so we can see ourselves and others more kindly?

I invite you to join me in this place of brave vulnerability and allow your creative self to make the best of life and your human-ness in the place you find yourself. Will you come too? Paint, draw, make, live, build, design but powerfully allow 'I Be' to resonate from your life. Gratefully open your gift so we can all share the light and joy you will be.

If you want to come with us to this lovely landscape then you are most welcome. Come tell of the new and good that you choose for your life among friends. Come share words of encouragement and truth together with us all.

We are blessed, all of us. We are human, all of us. We be.

> Now I am
> as I am
> and that is all I can be today.
>
> The finding of myself fully
> as I will be when I pass from this life,
> is a process that cannot happen until that time.
>
> I have the whole of my life
> to become the 'who' that I will be,
> without life's experience
> I will not know
> that version of myself.
>
> That version of 'me'
> will come from within
> and shine out from my inner sense of self.
> That 'I' that I am
> when I am in my quiet, gentle place
> with no words.

www.ingramcontent.com/pod-product-compliance
Lightning Source LLC
Chambersburg PA
CBHW071929290426
44110CB00013B/1538